Brands We Know

# Kellogg's

By Sara Green

Bellwether Media • Minneapolis, MN

Jump into the cockpit and take flight with *Pilot* books. Your journey will take you on high-energy adventures as you learn about all that is wild, weird, fascinating, and fun!

This edition first published in 2015 by Bellwether Media, Inc.

No part of this publication may be reproduced in whole or in part without written permission of the publisher.
For information regarding permission, write to Bellwether Media, Inc.,
Attention: Permissions Department,
5357 Penn Avenue South, Minneapolis, MN 55419.

Library of Congress Cataloging-in-Publication Data

Green, Sara, 1964- author.
 Kellogg's / by Sara Green.
     pages cm. -- (Pilot: Brands We Know)
 Includes bibliographical references and index.
 Summary: "Engaging images accompany information about the
Kellogg Company. The combination of high-interest subject matter
and narrative text is intended for students in grades 3 through 7"--
Provided by publisher.
 Audience: 7-12.
 Audience: Grades 3-7.
 ISBN 978-1-62617-207-4 (hardcover : alk. paper)
 1. Kellogg Company--History--Juvenile literature. 2. Kellogg, W. K.
(Will Keith), 1860-1951--Juvenile literature. 3. Kellogg, John Harvey,
1852-1943--Juvenile literature. 4. Breakfast cereals--United States--
History--Juvenile literature. I. Title.
 TP434.G74 2015
 338.7'664756'09--dc23
                              2014038659

Printed in the United States of America, North Mankato, MN.

# Table of Contents

What Is Kellogg's?....................................4

The Kellogg Brothers ..............................6

The King of Cereal ................................12

A Worldwide Brand ..............................14

A History of Giving.................................18

Kellogg's Timeline .................................20

Glossary ...................................................22

To Learn More.........................................23

Index.........................................................24

# What Is Kellogg's?

Every morning, millions of people sit down at the breakfast table to enjoy a bowl of cereal. Some favorites include Rice Krispies, Special K, and Frosted Flakes. The Kellogg Company makes these cereals and many more. This company helps people start their days with easy, healthy, and delicious breakfasts!

The Kellogg Company is a food **manufacturing** company based in Battle Creek, Michigan. It is the world's largest ready-to-eat cereal company. It also makes frozen foods and snacks such as waffles and crackers. In total, the company makes around 1,600 different kinds of food. Each day, people in more than 180 countries eat food made by the Kellogg Company. In 2013, it made more than $14 billion in sales! This makes Kellogg's one of the most popular **brands** in the world.

# By the Numbers

worth
**$22.5 billion**
in 2014

**18**
countries that make
Kellogg's products

more than
**16 billion**
raisins in boxes of
Raisin Bran sold in 2013

more than
**30,000**
employees

**139.7 million**
boxes of Frosted Flakes
sold in 2013

**10**
pounds (4.5 kilograms) of
cereal eaten by the average
American per year

# The Kellogg Brothers

People have not always eaten cereal for breakfast. Before 1900, people ate eggs, potatoes, or **porridge** in the morning. Meat, such as bacon and sausage, was also usually on the menu. The Kellogg brothers helped make cereal the popular breakfast food it is today.

John Harvey Kellogg was born on February 26, 1852, in Tyrone, Michigan. When John was about 4 years old, the Kellogg family moved to Battle Creek, Michigan. John's brother, Will Keith, known as W.K., was born there on April 7, 1860. The Kelloggs were members of the Seventh-day Adventist Church. Members of this religion follow rigid diet rules. They only eat healthy foods. They eat little sugar and almost no meat. The Kellogg boys grew up following these rules. This lifestyle led John to become interested in health. He studied medicine and became a doctor in 1875. In 1876, he was hired to run a hospital in Battle Creek. John renamed it the Battle Creek **Sanitarium**. It became known as the San.

Battle Creek Sanitarium

Will Keith "W.K." Kellogg

John Harvey Kellogg

# The Nation's Breakfast

1910s tagline for Kellogg's Corn Flakes

John believed poor diets caused people to get sick. He thought healthy food would cure them. John began to experiment with ways to make healthy breakfast food. Around 1880, he created a cereal from toasted wheat, oats, and corn. He called it Granola. This cereal was very hard. Many patients could not chew it. Then, in 1894, John and W.K. created the first flaked cereal. It was made from wheat. The flakes were tasty and easy to chew. The brothers soon figured out how to make flaked cereal from other grains, including toasted corn.

The patients liked eating corn flakes for breakfast. The San also began selling corn flakes to patients when they returned home. This gave W.K. an idea. The brothers could sell corn flakes to all people, not just former San patients. He also wanted to add sugar to make the cereal taste better. John disagreed with both ideas. He was happy with the way things were.

In 1906, W.K. started his own cereal company. It was called the Battle Creek Toasted Corn Flake Company. W.K.'s business and leadership skills made the company a success. Soon, millions of people were eating Toasted Corn Flakes for breakfast.

John was not happy about W.K.'s success. He believed W.K. had stolen his ideas. So John started another cereal company. He called it the Kellogg Food Company. In response, W.K. changed the name of his company to the Kellogg Toasted Corn Flake Company. His **signature** was on every cereal box to set his cereal apart from his brother's. The brothers began to fight even more. Both wanted sole **rights** to the Kellogg name. They went to court  to settle the matter. In time, W.K. won. Defeated, John changed his company's name to the Battle Creek Food Company. But it did not do as well as W.K.'s company, and the brothers never spoke again.

W.K. KELLOGG
FOUNDATION

258

## Trusted Friends

W.K. was blind for the last 14 years of his life. However, he stayed involved with the company and foundation. He attended all his meetings with a pet German Shepherd at his side.

# The King of Cereal

W.K. proved to be a **marketing** genius. He created clever magazine **advertisements** and gave away free samples of his cereal. He gained many customers this way. In 1922, W.K. renamed the company again. He called it the Kellogg Company. Soon, new Kellogg's cereals appeared on the market. W.K.'s signature was still on each box. In 1928, Rice Krispies was introduced. People enjoyed hearing the cereal pop when they poured milk on it. In 1929, the Kellogg Company began to use the **slogan** "Snap! Crackle! Pop!" to advertise Rice Krispies.

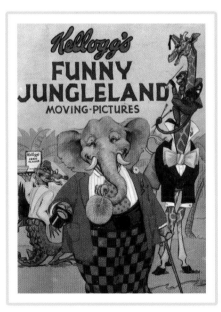

### Cereal Surprises

In 1910, W.K. Kellogg was the first to introduce prizes with boxes of cereal. The first prize was a picture book called *Funny Jungleland Moving Pictures*. Customers received it at the store when they bought two boxes of Kellogg's Toasted Corn Flakes.

# Put a Tiger on Your Team!

1950s tagline for Frosted Flakes

In the 1950s, the company introduced some of its most popular cereals. These included Corn Pops, Cocoa Krispies, and Special K. Tony the Tiger also appeared as the **mascot** for the new Frosted Flakes cereal. He was an instant hit! The 1960s saw even more growth. During this decade, the Kellogg Company launched Froot Loops, Apple Jacks, Frosted Mini-Wheats, and Pop-Tarts toaster pastries. People loved them all!

# A Worldwide Brand

Over time, the Kellogg Company continued to grow. The company still makes cereal and Pop-Tarts. Nutri-Grain cereal bars and Eggo frozen waffles have also become top sellers. Today, the company makes other kinds of food besides breakfast food. In 1999, the Kellogg Company bought MorningStar Farms. This company makes **vegetarian** food. Two years later, Kellogg's bought the Keebler Company. It makes cookies, crackers, and other snacks. Then in 2012, the Kellogg Company bought Pringles, a brand famous for its potato crisps.

**A Toaster Treat**
Kellogg's Pop-Tarts toaster pastries were the company's top-selling product in the 1990s.

The Kellogg Company still prides itself on making **nutritious** food. For this reason, many Kellogg's products contain extra **vitamins** and fiber to make them healthier. Some cereals are especially low in sugar and salt. The Kellogg Company also makes **gluten-free** food for people who cannot eat wheat. The company was one of the first food manufacturers to put ingredient labels on their packages. This allows customers to choose the foods that are best for them.

Today, Kellogg's foods are popular all over the world. Travelers may find that their favorite cereal has another name in other countries. This is because of language and culture differences. For example, Cocoa Krispies is called Choco Krispis in Colombia. In England, people eat Ricicles instead of Frosted Rice Krispies.

People also have different food preferences depending on where they live. For this reason, the Kellogg Company makes a variety of foods in countries around the world. In Canada, people enjoy All-Bran Strawberry Bites for breakfast. All-Bran Flakes come in chocolate in Italy and Spain. South Africans enjoy a fruit-flavored rice cereal called Strawberry Pops. In India, people can buy Corn Flakes made with mangos, bananas, or strawberries!

## Traveling With Kellogg's

Kellogg's food has gone to faraway places. In the 1930s, Admiral Richard E. Byrd ate Kellogg's food on his journey to the South Pole. In 1969, astronauts on the Apollo 11 ate Kellogg's food during their mission to the moon.

# Cereals Around the World

| United States Brand Name | International Brand Name | Region |
|---|---|---|
| Cocoa Krispies | Choco Krispis | Latin America |
| | Choco Krispies | Europe |
| | Coco Pops | Europe, Asia, Australia, New Zealand, and South Africa |
| Frosted Flakes | Frosties | Europe, Asia, Australia, New Zealand, and South Africa |
| | Zucaritas | Latin America |
| | Sucrilhos | Brazil |
| | Corn Frosty | Japan |
| Frosted Mini-Wheats | Mini Max | The United Kingdom |
| Frosted Rice Krispies | Ricicles | The United Kingdom |
| Honey Smacks | Smacks | Europe |
| Krave | Tresor | Europe |
| Raisin Bran | Sultana Bran | Australia, New Zealand, and the United Kingdom |
| Rice Krispies | Rice Bubbles | Australia and New Zealand |

# A History of Giving

The Kellogg Company has a long history of helping others. In 1930, W.K. started the W.K. Kellogg **Foundation**. He wanted to use his money to improve the health and education of children around the world. Today, the foundation helps children and their communities in many ways. One project provides free preschool to children in parts of Michigan. Another works to increase the number of children attending elementary school in Haiti.

The Kellogg Company also cares about the environment. The first box of Kellogg's cereal was made of recycled material. Today, almost all Kellogg's cereal boxes are made from 100 percent recycled material. The company also helps protect **rain forests**. Some of Kellogg's ingredients come from the rain forests of **tropical** countries. Kellogg's has promised to buy only from companies that protect the forest as they harvest. This promise will help preserve rain forests and their animals for years to come. Every day, the Kellogg's Company works to keep Earth and its people healthy.

# Let's Make Today Great

2010s tagline

## Feeding America

The Kellogg Company also donates food to Feeding America. This organization seeks to end hunger in the United States. Since 2004, Kellogg's has donated more than 200 million pounds (91 million kilograms) of food.

Our Children. Our Mission. Our Future.

W.K. KELLOGG FOUNDATION

W. K. KELLOGG FOUNDATION

One Michigan Avenue East

# Kellogg's Timeline

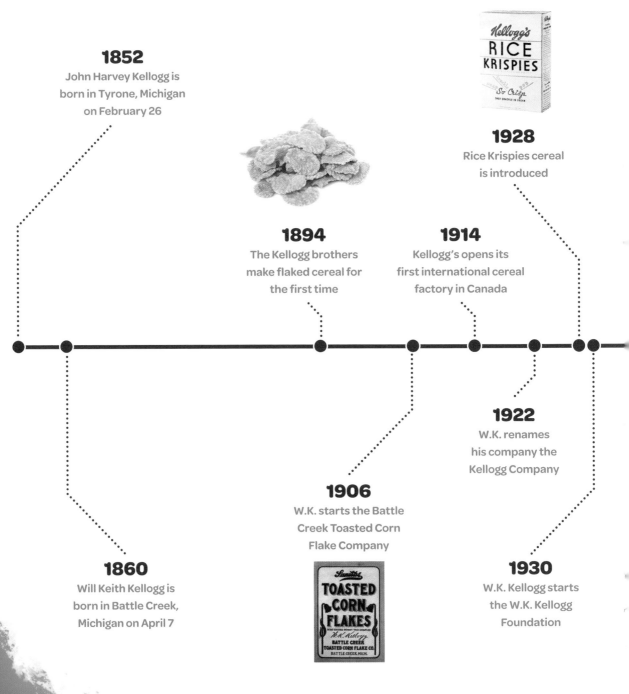

**1852**
John Harvey Kellogg is born in Tyrone, Michigan on February 26

**1928**
Rice Krispies cereal is introduced

**1894**
The Kellogg brothers make flaked cereal for the first time

**1914**
Kellogg's opens its first international cereal factory in Canada

**1922**
W.K. renames his company the Kellogg Company

**1906**
W.K. starts the Battle Creek Toasted Corn Flake Company

**1860**
Will Keith Kellogg is born in Battle Creek, Michigan on April 7

**1930**
W.K. Kellogg starts the W.K. Kellogg Foundation

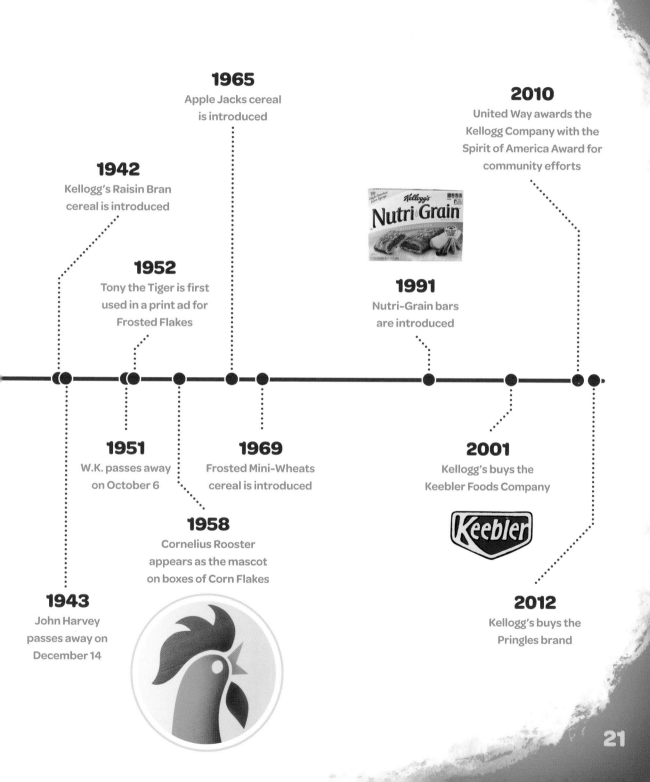

**1965**

Apple Jacks cereal
is introduced

**2010**

United Way awards the
Kellogg Company with the
Spirit of America Award for
community efforts

**1942**

Kellogg's Raisin Bran
cereal is introduced

**1952**

Tony the Tiger is first
used in a print ad for
Frosted Flakes

**1991**

Nutri-Grain bars
are introduced

**1951**

W.K. passes away
on October 6

**1969**

Frosted Mini-Wheats
cereal is introduced

**2001**

Kellogg's buys the
Keebler Foods Company

**1958**

Cornelius Rooster
appears as the mascot
on boxes of Corn Flakes

**1943**

John Harvey
passes away on
December 14

**2012**

Kellogg's buys the
Pringles brand

# Glossary

**advertisements**—notices and messages that announce or promote something

**brands**—categories of products all made by the same company

**foundation**—an institution that provides funds to charitable organizations

**gluten-free**—contains no wheat

**manufacturing**—making raw materials into products that people use

**marketing**—promoting and selling a product

**mascot**—an animal or object used as a symbol by a group or company

**nutritious**—healthy

**porridge**—a food made from boiling grains in milk or water

**rain forests**—thick, green forests that receive a lot of rain

**rights**—the legal ability to use a certain name or product

**sanitarium**—a place where sick people go to get better

**signature**—the special way a person writes his or her name

**slogan**—a short, memorable phrase used in advertising

**tropical**—having a hot, wet climate

**vegetarian**—made without meat

**vitamins**—natural substances found in food that help the body stay healthy

# To Learn More

## AT THE LIBRARY

Epstein, Rachel. *W.K. Kellogg: Generous Genius*. New York, N.Y.: Children's Press, 2000.

Mattern, Joanne. *The Kellogg Family: Breakfast Cereal Pioneers*. Edina, Minn.: ABDO Pub. Co., 2011.

Wyckoff, Edwin Brit. *The Cornflake King: W.K. Kellogg and His Amazing Cereal*. Berkeley Heights, N.J.: Enslow Elementary, 2011.

## ON THE WEB

Learning more about Kellogg's is as easy as 1, 2, 3.

1. Go to www.factsurfer.com.

2. Enter "Kellogg's" into the search box.

3. Click the "Surf" button and you will see a list of related web sites.

With factsurfer.com, finding more information is just a click away.

# Index

Apollo 11, 16

Battle Creek, Michigan, 4, 6

Battle Creek Sanitarium, 6, 9

brands, 14

by the numbers, 5

Byrd, Richard E. (Admiral), 16

charity, 18, 19

company names, 10, 12

Feeding America, 19

Frosted Flakes, 4, 5, 13, 17

history, 6, 9, 10, 11, 12, 13, 14, 15

international products, 16, 17

Kellogg, John Harvey, 6, 7, 9, 10

Kellogg, Will Keith, 6, 7, 9, 10, 11, 12, 18

Kellogg's Corn Flakes, 8, 9, 10, 12, 16

marketing, 12

mascot, 13

nutrition, 6, 9, 15

Pop-Tarts, 13, 14, 15

products, 4, 5, 9, 10, 12, 13, 14, 15, 16, 17

Rice Krispies, 4, 12, 17

sales, 4

Seventh-day Adventist Church, 6

sustainability, 18

taglines, 8, 11, 12, 13, 19

timeline, 20-21

W.K. Kellogg Foundation, 11, 18

worth, 5

The images in this book are reproduced through the courtesy of: Charles Brutlag, table of contents; Jon Eppard, p. 4 (left); digitalreflections, pp. 4 (middle), 13 (middle), 14 (left), 21 (top, bottom right); Lunasee Studios, p. 4 (right); Joshua Resnick, p. 5; United States Library of Congress/ Public Domain, p. 6; Bettmann/ Corbis, p. 7 (left); Library of Congress, p. 7 (right); andersphoto, p. 8; Volosina, p. 9 (left); Lovely Bird, p. 9 (right); Richard B. Levine/ Newscom, p. 10; W.K. Kellogg Foundation, p. 11; Louise Volper, p. 12; dcwcreations, p. 13 (left, right); George W. Bailey, p. 14 (middle); Emka74, p. 14 (right); Associated Press/ AP Images, p. 15; Madlen, p. 16; Mediablitzimages/ Alamy, p. 17 (left); Handout/ KRT/ Newscom, p. 17 (middle); Jon Le-Bon, p. 17 (right); Dennis MacDonald/ Alamy, p. 19; Davydenko Yuliia, p. 20 (top left); Print Collector/ Contributor/ Getty Images, p. 20 (top right); Kellogg's Company/ Wikipedia Public Domain, p. 20 (bottom); Tony Ding/ Corbis, p. 21 (bottom left).